A Pair of Arrow Back Chairs Flank an 18th Century Chest
—All Refinished According to the Methods
Outlined In This Book.

WILLIAM FARWELL

EASY DOES IT
FURNITURE RESTORATION
the Vermont Way

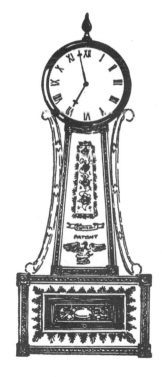

CHARLES E. TUTTLE Co., Inc.
Publishers   Rutland, Vermont

Published by the Charles E. Tuttle Company, Inc.
of Rutland, Vermont & Tokyo, Japan
with editorial offices at
Suido 1-chome, 2-6, Bunkyo-ku, Tokyo, Japan

Copyright in Japan, 1968 by Charles E. Tuttle Co., Inc.

Library of Congress Catalog Card No. 70-113905

International Standard Book No. 0-8048-0156-8

Photographs by Robert Bennett & Sherman Howe

PRINTED IN JAPAN

To the charming young lady whom I met on a summer's evening and drove the long way home.

CONTENTS

FOREWORD

Your author represents everything that proper New Englanders consider bad. He firmly believes that most great accomplishments and real pleasures come at night. So he insists on sitting up for at least half of it. He detests getting up in the morning, his idea of the crack of dawn being approximately 10 A. M.

He is inherently lazy, always looking for a way to do something easier and more quickly. His furniture finish, FARWELL'S FINEST was concocted, after some months of experimentation, to take the place of French Polish. The French polishing method of finishing furniture, so long used in England and on the Continent, produces the finest finish known. But, as done by the old-timers, it requires practice for which the average individual does not have time.

SANTASH, to remove spots from finished furniture, was made to replace some rather fabulous stuff made on special order, at considerable expense, by a distant laboratory.

The idea of designing and marketing FARWELL'S HAND SCRAPER FOR WOOD suggested itself because so many folks dislike the messy, smelly and sometimes dangerous liquid removers.

Not all his fanciful schemes have worked, nor have they met with complete approval of "his sisters and his brothers and his cousins and his aunts". But the modus operandi set forth in this book has been tried out for years. It works! If you have an interest in doing fine restoration work, it will save you time, labor and produce satisfying results.

INTRODUCTION

Restoring work done at home can be fun, giving real personal satisfaction from the results and at small cost. Or it can be confusing, with discouraging results and at considerable expense. We have read directions for this sort of work which are as complicated, and as confusing, as would be a treatise on How to Become a Surgeon in Ten Easy Lessons.

There are certain occasional jobs in restoration work which can be done best with mechanical contrivances. In any community there are competent wood working or machine shops equipped to do this work well, quickly and at small expense. Fine restoration work is hand work, be it amateur or professional. We take pride in the fact that, over the years, many fine antiques, some from a considerable distance, have been brought to The Shop of William Farwell for restoration work. We have one electric sander, rarely used, and no other mechanical tool.

We outline in this book methods which are practical and can be done with a minimum of equipment and supplies. If, in each case, our method is carefully followed, it will result in a really professional job. This we know from years of experience. We recommend our own products because we believe they are the best for the job at hand. We recommend other products which we have used and found most satisfactory. For the convenience of our readers, we include a list of necessary products and where they may easily be obtained. We include sections on specialized work about which there is not too much readily available information, such as gilding and piano refinishing. We avoid directions for work which is too complicated or not adaptable to cellar or kitchen, such as, for instance, installing genuine rush seats.

NOTA BENE and proceed. And may you dream of a crowded auction gallery with the bids going up by leaps and bounds on a little wash stand restored by you!

WELL WORTH THE EXPENDITURE OF ALMOST INFINITE RESTORATION TIME
ARE EXAMPLES OF SUCH SUPERLATIVE DESIGN AND CRAFTSMANSHIP
AS THIS QUEEN ANNE CHAIR AND CHERRY CANDLESTAND FROM
THE COLLECTION OF THE AUTHOR.

WHAT IS IT WORTH —
AND IS IT WORTH REFINISHING?

We are not here concerned with the appraised value of antique furniture. Some old pieces we own may have little market value but very great sentimental worth. Or we may have pieces which combine market and sentimental value. We are the proud possessors of a Hepplewhite cherry swell front chest with string inlay and medallions of bird's eye maple in the drawer fronts. This piece has better than average market value. Sentimentally it was part of the furnishing of the new home of Patience Walker when she married our direct ancestor, Lemuel Farwell, about 1790. Items to which great sentiment is attached are restored and cared for without thought of time or cost. But, disregarding sentiment, any honest professional restorer will advise against work on any piece of furniture the cost of which exceeds the amount by which the value of the piece is enhanced. This is a rather good rule for the amateur restorer to follow. In acquiring things by purchase, try to select items which will justify your considerable time and some material expense in restoring. Try to consider the design and the wood more than the condition. A piece with grace and charm and of beautiful wood may be worthy of an infinite number of repairs. We remember a graceful cherry table which required 26 elliptical patches (see Section III, REPAIRS) to make presentable the top. On the other hand a piece with no particularly attractive lines and made of horrible green poplar wood would never look right, no matter how many hours of work or what number of stains and finishes are used.

Generally speaking, the earlier the period the more apt is the piece to be attractive. Surely the delicate lines of Sheraton, Hepplewhite and Adam possess more beauty than, for the most part, the gross design of Empire. And some of the still earlier Queen Anne pieces are the very ultimate of grace, charm and beauty.

Section II

WOODS

Trees — a blanket covering our mountains and hills. In the winter the gray of weather beaten boards, with, perhaps, a touch of the pale lavendar of early flint glass. In spring pale greens, ever darkening. In the fall yellows, burnt orange and flaming red. Always a sprinkling of dark evergreens with bits of white from the birches. Here and there the swath of a power line or ski run, occasionally an outcropping of bare rock ledge.

Work and war take us to far places, but there is always the thought of our wooded Vermont hills, bringing a mixture of homesickness and strength. This is a wonderful and lasting sentiment for Vermonters, but the really big trees have almost all been long since cut.

First growth timber seasoned by long exposure to good air and sunshine together with beautiful long wide boards of heavy, dense grain woods, contributed to the unhurried work, pride of accomplishment and the inspiration of the great cabinet maker designers which produced American 18th and early 19th furniture of grace, charm and lasting value.

Today, first growth timber has all but disappeared, dense Santo Domingo mahogany is found only in old pieces, cherry is not even cut and sawed the same and the color and grain is nothing compared to that in the really old boards. So, for inlays and other repairs we try to get pieces of old wood. (See Section III, REPAIRS.)

There is a great deal of talk, too much talk, about patina. It is what Wallace Nutting called, "this pitter-patter about patina". Patina is a surface mellowing and coloring caused mostly by years of exposure to the light and enhanced by the original French polish finish. Light woods, such as pine and maple slightly darken, pigmented woods such as mahogany and walnut fade to a beautiful tone. "Of fine faded mahogany" is an expression often found in descriptions of individual pieces in sales and auction catalogues. In finishing over or caring for pieces of exceptional design and rare color,

12

surface imperfections are left undisturbed, because scraping, or even light sanding, will disturb this fine, old color. But a stand or table covered with penetrating or varnish stains of horrible color, or a battered chair of inherent good lines but covered with layers of paint, most certainly possesses no patina. They may be scraped, sanded and finished with impunity. In the case of old cherry a fine color is all the way through the wood. Light woods which have been covered with stain or paint may seem too light when scraped and sanded. They may be finished this way and left for the natural light to mellow. Or they may be mellowed by application of a light, thin stain. (See Section V, STAINING).

Woods or veneers for repair work (see Section III, REPAIRS) may be obtained by picking up odds and ends from antique dealers, professional antique restoration shops or at auctions. We purchased a battered old cherry table at an auction for five dollars. The one good leaf was sawed in two and made a fine top for a cherry pedestal candle stand to replace a modern top which had been added. One leg was re-turned to replace a missing leg of a fine old piece and there is still enough good old cherry wood left and waiting to be used for repairs. String inlays, medallions of exotic woods and the like may be obtained from reliable dealers. (See list, rear of book.)

A Collection of Old Woods Useful for Restoration Work.

REPAIRS

Unfortunately we do not know how to drive a nail straight, hang storm windows, repair door locks, push a lawn mower, work clipping shears or shovel snow. Possibly this comes about through lack of intelligence. But we must confess that we have done some work on intricate marquetry which met the mutual approval of the adjuster for a great insurance company and the assured. And once we threw a female client into practical ecstacy with our work on the top rail of a Louis XV fauteuil which had been considerably damaged in an argument between a moving van and a cement bridge abutment. Or maybe, with storm windows, et cetera, it is just avoiding the issue, like Grandpa Stowell. Someone asked him why he never tended the family coal burning furnace. His reply, "I can't. I don't know where it's located!". We have tried to make the section on repairs to antiques intelligible. If you have some liking for the work, we predict success.

In restoring antique furniture the general rule is to repair, not replace. A table with top or drop leaf repaired is more attractive, and decidedly more valuable, than one with a new center board or leaf. The same holds true of the bulbous legs and stretchers of a Windsor chair; the back splat, top rail or arms of Queen Anne, Chippendale or chairs of other periods and designs; and of the turned or square tapered legs of stands.

A rather common job required is the repair of cracks by the making of a new glue joint in table or stand tops. The old timers did this by folding over the two opposing parts like the leaves of a book, clamping them together very tightly and preparing the edges to be joined with an extremely sharp plane having an infinitesimal dip at the center. Then when the two parts were unfolded, the edges covered with glue and brought together with long clamps, there would be greater pressure toward each end, resulting in a remarkably tight joint. This is beyond the skill of the average worker at home. Nor is it necessary. Any competent wood working shop will run the parts to be joined through an edger, glue them, clamp them and turn out a fine, tight, lasting joint in short time and at little expense.

Surface repairs can and should be done at home. Light burns, small gouges, dents and imperfections can be scraped out (see Section IV. PREPARING THE SURFACE FOR FINISHING). We are not in favor of the use of plastic material in the repair of antiques, although it can be used to fill small nail holes. We recommend Duritite. It drys hard, sands nicely. Use a neutral color and stain to match the surrounding wood after finishing (see Section V, STAINING).

For surface burns, gouges too deep to scrape out, and for large holes, use an inlay. You have perhaps seen table tops repaired with square or round plugs. They stick out like a sore thumb! To make properly a repair of this sort, mark out with a pencil, around the hole or gouge, an elongated, elliptical design. Take this off with tracing paper. Then with an X-Acto knife cut out the design you have penciled to a little depth, making the edges vertical and the bottom flat. Then, using the design on your tracing paper, cut out a thin piece of wood very slightly larger than the hole which has been cut. With the flat side of a half round wood file, taper slightly the edges of this piece. Gradually work a fit to the hole so that the repair piece slips into the hole about half its thickness. Next apply glue to hole and to sides and bottom of repair piece. Fix repair piece into hole tightly by pounding with a wooden mallet or block of wood. When glue has set, sand repair piece even with surrounding surface. If old wood of approximate color and grain (see Section II, WOODS) is used for the patch, the finished results will be what looks like a natural swirl or knot in the surface repaired and not a patch. We recommend for this job (and also for regluing chair joints, etc.) a cold, plastic resin glue, such as ELMER'S GLUE-ALL, put out by the Borden Company.

To repair or replace the old, thick veneers (see

Section II, WOODS) use the same method as described in the preceding paragraph. However, for gluing veneers in any position we recommend WELDWOOD CONTACT CEMENT. In this case the spot to be repaired and the veneer patch are well coated with the cement and left apart for about twenty minutes, or until they feel dry to the touch. Then the repair piece is pressed in with the thumb and fingers, for a tight, lasting bond. This is especially advantageous on the top or sides or pieces where it would be difficult to use clamps.

Chair strechers, legs, etc. can be reglued with the cold resin glue and brought together and held tightly until the glue sets by using clothes line, together with a wooden dowel or handle of a hammer or screwdriver, like a tourniquet. This method avoids the purchase of various sizes of clamps.

Bulbous turnings of chair and table legs can be repaired by making a flat surface with the flat side of a half round wood file, then gluing on a block of wood. When glue has set, the repair piece can be shaped with the flat and round sides of the file, then smoothed with sand paper.

Make all repairs with wood and glue, not nails or screws. Wood is, to a certain extent, like blotting paper. It expands and contracts with changes in humidity. The steel in nails and screws remains the same size. Consequently, as the wood around them expands and contracts, they gradually loosen and have to be removed or, in the case of nails, dug out, leaving unsightly marks. If a repair made with glue loosens or gives away, it is a simple matter to reglue without disfiguring the piece.

PREPARING THE SURFACE FOR FINISHING

"If it is worth doing, it is worth doing, or knowing how to do, yourself".

It is trite but true that a surface well prepared is the foundation for a fine finish. By using a little extra time and care, you will be more than well repaid by the end results.

Old paints, stain, stain varnish and all other previous finishes are easily and cleanly removed with a fine scraper like FARWELL'S HAND SCRAPER FOR WOOD. This simple hand tool of specially hardened steel has edges hollow ground like a skate blade. It takes off a very fine shaving (just the depth of the hollow ground). As each shaving is of the same thickness, it results in a surface which requires a minimum of sanding to prepare the surface for finishing. The controlled edge eliminates any danger of gouging the wood (as sometimes happens when scraping with glass).

The scraper has opposing ends which are slightly curved. There are four edges which can be used. Any part of the straight edges can be used for scraping chair legs, table legs, stretchers, spindles and stiles. For scraping flat or incurvate surfaces, the scraping is done with the edges of the scraper toward the ends which curve upward.

The edges of the scraper will not hold their sharpness forever, although they last much longer than any scraping device we have used over the years. The tool can be sharpened anywhere that skates are sharpened (or see SCRAPER SHARPENING SERVICE, listed at rear of book).

There are decided advantages in using a scraper rather than a liquid remover. The dry shavings from a scraper can be easily cleaned up, brushed from the clothes. Liquid removers, for the most part, are messy to handle resulting in the inevitable spots on clothes which are hard to remove. Not all removers are combustible and give off toxic fumes, but many of them are fire hazards and do have poisonous fumes. Also, any liquid strong enough to dissolve old paint and stain has a tendency to drive part of it further into the wood. This results in an extra amount of sanding, or even scraping. Not incidentally, the cost of a long lasting scraper is less than the cost of one gallon of most paint removers.

Bamboo turnings of Windsor chairs and all turnings of table and chair legs cannot be properly cleaned with either scraper or remover. Paint, stain and old finish has sunk unusually deep in these turnings because they are the head grain of the wood. A half round wood file, using both the flat and curved sides, is an excellent means of cleaning out these turnings. Fine carvings must be treated carefully. While it takes a little time, we believe the safest method is to soak the old finish off with denatured alcohol, using a brass suede leather brush to clean out the old finish as it softens. The brass brush is stiff enough to do the job without, at the same time, damaging the details of the carving.

All scraped parts are sanded to be made ready for finishing. We recommend ADALOX OPENKOTE paper made by the Behr-Manning division of Norton Company. It is hard, clogs much less than most papers and can be further kept clear by brushing with a suede leather brush. For a really fine surface, use a medium grit paper first and then a fine grit.

On table or stand tops, an extra fine surface results from wetting the surface with alcohol to raise the grain and then, when dry, a final sanding with a very fine grit paper. To get a fine finish on a table top of open grain wood, such as mahogany or walnut, the grain must be filled. This can be done with an infinite amount of padding finish or many, many coats of brush finish. But the process is too long. Fill the grain with a neutral colored filler stained to match the particular piece of wood (see Section V, STAINING). This is more satisfactory than purchasing a colored filler which never seems to quite match the color of the wood. Let the filler down with turpentine to brushing consistency. Apply with a rather stiff brush with the grain of the wood. Let dry a few minutes until the surface takes on a dull look. Then, with a rough cloth, such as burlap or turkish toweling, rub hard across the grain of the wood. This leaves the grain filled, the surface clear. Let dry over night and then sand lightly with a fine grit paper. You are now ready to apply finish.

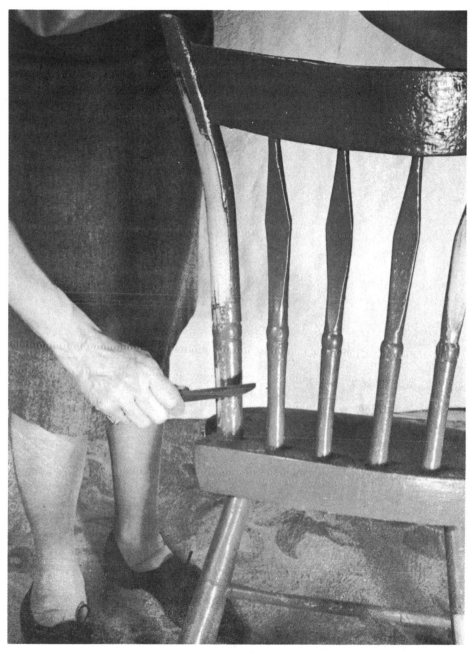

THE USE OF AN APPROPRIATE, WELL SHARPENED SCRAPER RELIEVES THE
TEDIUM OF REMOVING THE OLD FINISH FROM THE TURNED
PORTIONS OF THIS ARROW-BACK CHAIR.

STAINING

When we were very young, we were informed by our parents that only very bad women "painted their faces". At that early age we were not given any of the details as to what painted ladies did on the side to make them so wicked. Nowadays, of course, very lovely ladies of character beyond reproach do use a touch of artificial color. We recently congratulated a lady who had undergone a very delicate heart operation, remarking especially upon her wonderful complexion. Her reply, "But, of course, part of it can be purchased!" Well, anyway, maybe our early lessons prejudiced us against artificial color. So, generally speaking, we avoid staining in the restoration of antiques. The early country cabinet makers used whatever woods were available and not necessarily all the same wood in each piece. But as time has gone on, the woods have mellowed, lighter ones darkened, the pigmented woods faded, to make a delightful and interesting blend of colors. An old one drawer stand with a maple base, cherry top and perhaps a mahogany drawer front is far more attractive than the same stand stained in an attempt to make it look exactly all the same color.

Sometimes sizeable replacements have to be made or the original wood is not particularly attractive, such as poplar or basswood. Then we do have to stain. Just two colors in oil will give us, in different proportions, exactly the effect we desire. These are burnt umber—a fine brown—and burnt sienna—a pinky red. A mixture of these two colors will give us the effect of brown mahogany, red mahogany, cherry (light or dark) or any other shade we like. In making the stain, no oil should be added. Thin with pure spirits of turpentine and to each half pint of stain add three or four tablespoonsfuls of Japan drier. Mix quite thin and rub on with a cheesecloth pad. If the result is too dark, it may be lightened (immediately) with a pad soaked in turpentine.

Over hard woods the stain may be applied directly

to the sanded wood. Over soft woods, such as pine, poplar or basswood, the stain is apt to strike in unevenly with a streaked result hard to get out. So with soft woods it is better to brush on a coat, or maybe two coats, of thin orange shellac (25% shellac, 75% alcohol) and, when dry sand well with fine sandpaper. Then apply stain. Small repair inlays, or nail holes filled with Duratite, may be colored with a small, soft brush dipped in analine stain after the piece is finished with FARWELL'S FINEST. Analine stains take into our finish, oil stains do not. A mixture of Bismark Brown powder disolved in alcohol (making a bright red) and Nigrosine black powder dissolved, will, in different proportions, produce any color desired.

On ebonized pianos, edges worn through to the wood as well as accidental mars or gouges may be stained with Nigrosine black over our finish. Still better ask your piano dealer to get a small amount of black from the manufacturer. Maple, pine or butternut, if too light in color, can be mellowed by rubbing with burnt umber let down with turpentine. Add two or three tablespoons of Japan drier to each half pint. As with other stains made the same way, the shade can be lightened by rubbing (immediately) with a clean pad moistened with turpentine.

FINISHING

We remember a big kitchen, larger than most apartment living rooms, with a Glenwood coal range, set tubs of slate and, in one corner, a zinc lined box with pure spring water bubbling up. Here, during the day time, presided a lady who, at $4.00 per week, was not only a great cook but a loyal supporter and friend of the family. On many evenings the big kitchen became a workshop for finishing things made of wood. We watched our Dad as he worked, with a patience hard to comprehend, on a Windsor chair, a cherry stand or, perhaps, the fine walnut stock of a deer rifle. We smelled the good smell of the materials he was using and followed his operations. Occasionally they were interrupted by the jangling wall telephone bringing the news that Lord Brothers had a new pacer that looked pretty good for tomorrow's Free-for-All over the ice on the Winooski River, or the rumor that the strawberry roan mare, May Bird, entered in the green race by young Farwell, had raced before and there was going to be a protest. The thought of all these things brings on nostalgia and from all this comes our love of fine wood, beautifully finished.

There are many excellent finishing materials and various methods of applying them to produce the finest of finishes. We stress the use of our wood scraper and our finishing material because we believe them to be the best for "the purpose at hand". By "the purpose at hand" we mean the desire of people of intelligence to refinish a piece of furniture, or restore an antique, in their own cellar or kitchen in a reasonable length of time and without elaborate equipment. The folks we have in mind do not have a dust proof room, set of badger hair brushes, grinding wheels, hones, steel burnishers, edgers, electric sanders, mechanical buffers, et cetera, ad infinitum.

FARWELL'S FINEST gives all the results of the finest French finish without the practice and skill required to do it with the method used by the old-timers.

22

It is applied easily and quickly with a cheesecloth pad of convenient size. The pad is moistened with the finish and applied to the wood with a circular motion. This keeps the pad continuously moving while on the wood and avoids leaving press marks. The circular motions are made in any direction, paying no attention to the grain of the wood. The amount of finish needed is governed somewhat by the type of wood—old, punky pine, for instance, takes more than hard maple. One watches the surface of the wood (looking into the light) to determine when sufficient finish has been applied. Small, convenient sized areas are "rubbed up" before applying the finish on additional areas. No lap marks will show. In fact, if one is interrupted, a section of a table top may be left unfinished and the work completed another day. The stop and start will not show. An extra fine finish may be built up by application beyond the minimum requirement.

The average cellar or kitchen is not dust proof. Slow drying finishes applied by brush look great when first applied. But by the time the finish has set, the surface has acquired a pebbly effect from particles deposited from the air. Our finish has an alcohol base. As the finish is applied, the alcohol evaporates quickly while the resins in the finish are being spread upon the wood. There is absolutely no dust problem. In fact a chair when just finished with FARWELL'S FINEST is almost dry enough to use. With our finish there is no sanding between coats, no expensive brushes to purchase and to keep clean. Even the inexpensive cheesecloth pads can be kept in a vacuum can and used repeatedly before discarding.

Our personal preference is for a slightly dull finish rather than a shiny or high finish. If a very high final finish is desired, moisten very, very slightly a clean cheesecloth pad with drops of alcohol. Very gently rub the finished surface with this pad, going in the direction of the grain of the wood. A very fine dull finish is done by rubbing the finished surface with a pad of oooo (the finest) steel wool. This is just as effective as pumice powder and oil and much less messy.

23

In finishing turned table legs, stretchers, spindles, and legs of chairs, first apply the finish with the pad, then pull the pad apart and use like a shoe shining cloth. This is a quick and easy way to bring up a fine shine on turned parts. On carvings and ornate decorative parts sop in the finish with a quite wet pad. Them immediately brush with a fairly soft shoe shining brush.

An important use for FARWELL'S FINEST is over stencilled or hand painted decoration. Often the original finish over the decoration has crazed, the check marks going into the decoration itself. These marks cannot be sanded out because this would remove the decoration. Using our finish, these marks can be padded in, completely filling them, without disturbing the decoration and, at the same time, adding a protective coating of finish. This method can be used over the finest decoration. Some years back we had in our shop an Adam-Hepplewhite Pembroke table of mahogany completely veneered with satinwood. On the top were classic figures, on the legs garlands of pink rose buds, painted by that great 18th Century English artist, Angelica Kauffmann. This table was badly crazed, but the final result of our work was extremely satisfactory.

When the condition of a previous finish is such that it seems unnecessary to remove it, a satisfactory restoration job can be done with FARWELL'S FINEST. It "takes into" such finishes as shellac, varnish or oil. It cannot be used however, over a previous finish of lacquer. When restoring old finishes be sure they are first cleaned of dirty, oily film and especially of wax. Carbon tetra chloride is an excellent cleaning agent and it does remove wax.

People ask us, "Is your finish heat and alcohol proof?". It is not. It is a hard, permanent, long lasting finish that will stand a lot of wear. The resins in our finish do, as affected by the air, develop a certain resistance to alcohol. But it cannot be used, as are certain brush or sprayed applied finishes, for a sensational demonstration of pouring on grain alcohol or boiling water. But most accidents to fine furniture do not come from boiling water or grain alcohol. From our experience, it is more likely that the baby gives the table top a healthy wallop with a lead soldier, a toddler gets hold of an interesting nail file that makes perfectly fascinating scratches, or Papa gets into a heated discussion of the state of the economy or politics and his burning cigar or cigarette falls over and does quite a job on finished wood. No finish, no matter how hard, can stand this sort of treatment. Aforesaid blemishes in most finishes cannot be repaired without doing over a whole top or panel. A repaired spot is bound to show. With our finish the spot is scraped and sanded out and then the finish padded in. The repaired spot will, definitely, show no lap marks. Also, no finish will last forever. Arms of chairs and other places taking unusual wear will result in any finish wearing thin. Additional finish may be padded on to these areas with FARWELL'S FINEST. This is practically impossible to do with a brush applied finish.

On kitchen table tops that are regularly scrubbed, on dining table tops, if you are not going to be careful about hot dishes, and on coffee table tops a very hard finish is helpful. We give directions for applying three finishes, all excellent for these particular purposes.

There is no table top finish finer than an oil finish. But to do it right, you must have the patience of Job, time galore and plenty of energy. After the surface is prepared for finishing, start by rubbing a mixture of 2/3 boiled linseed oil and 1/3 pure spirits of turpentine into the wood with a soft cloth. Apply all the oil the wood will absorb — this will take from five to twenty minutes, depending on nature of the wood, temperature of oil and room. Wipe off excess oil and polish from ten to twenty minutes (coarse material, such as turkish toweling, is excellent for this purpose). Let stand for two days and repeat. From four or five to twelve coats of oil are needed to bring out a lustre that gives a soft, satiny effect. Allow more time between each successive coat. Between the last coats allow at least a week — longer if it is not dry weather. A last finishing touch for a really super job is to rub the whole surface with the palm of your hand.

For a brush applied hard varnish, we like a plastic base spar varnish. After the surface of the table top is prepared (and filled if an open grain wood) apply a coat of varnish full strength. Some prefer the first coat somewhat let down with turpentine. We prefer full strength. There are different theories about brushes. Some say use an inexpensive brush and discard it; others say use a very fine (which means expensive) brush. Take your choice. But we have never used a brush that failed to let loose, occasionally, a bristle or two. Watch this closely and pick out loose bristles immediately. If you use a fine brush, clean first with turpentine, then wash in warm water and Ivory soap, immediately after using. Brushing varnishes are difficult at best because they collect dust particles from the air. Without a dust proof room, the best bet is to apply varnish late at night with less moving about in the household and the heat turned down (heat waves stir up dust particles in the air). Let the first coat set for three days. Then go over it lightly with 360-A wet or dry finishing paper (used dry). Repeat operation for the second coat. After this has set for three days, sprinkle top liberally with cold water. Then sand to a fine smoothness with 360-A finishing paper soaked in water. Repeat operation for the third coat. When this has set three days, sprinkle with cold water and sand lightly with 500-A finishing paper soaked in water. Dry surface thoroughly and do a final finish by rubbing the surface with a bat of 0000 (the finest) steel wool soaked in a light oil. If more of a shine is desired, rub surface with a mixture of rotten stone and light oil applied with a felt pad.

FARWELL'S HARDTOP produces the final effect of a hard brush-applied varnish, but no brushes are necessary and the finish is less inclined to take on dust particles while drying. After the surface is fine sanded very smooth (and filled if an open grain wood) wipe on the HARDTOP with a cheesecloth pad. Use smooth, even strokes with the grain of the wood. Do not leave

26

a thick coat on the wood. Let dry for at least two days. Repeat the operation. After second coat has dried, smooth the surface with medium steel wool. Then apply third coat. After this has thoroughly dried, finish with a bat of fine steel wool (either ooo or oooo) soaked in any light oil. This is the final finish we like. If you desire a higher finish, rub the surface with a felt pad, soaked in light oil and sprinkled with rotten stone.

Burns, gouges etc. can be repaired by scraping, sanding and then finishing the spot as you previously finished the whole surface.

HARDTOP is very resistant to heat, water and alcohol. A cloth soaked in straight alcohol can be rubbed on the finished surface without any effect to the finish.

An old time physician once told us that if he were starting practice all over again, he would prefer common salt and water to alcohol. Well, in our work, we prefer cheap cheesecloth to the most expensive fabric ever woven. A cheesecloth pad is the start and usually the finish of all our fine finishing work. Here is how we make what seems to us the most convenient pad. We cut off about fourteen inches from a three thickness, nine inch wide bolt of cheesecloth. We just barely fold over the rough ends and then make two folds of equal width. This gives us a pad about three and a half inches wide on either side. This pad is then folded twice and is ready for use. It can be reversed to use the opposite side. It can be pulled apart to use like a shoe shine cloth on turned parts. If kept in a vacuum tin, it will remain soft and usable for a considerable time. There is nothing in either of our finishing materials harmful to the skin. After using FARWELL'S FINEST clean hands with denatured alcohol; after HARDTOP use turpentine. However, to avoid cleaning sticky hands and a certain amount of manicuring, wear thin rubber gloves.

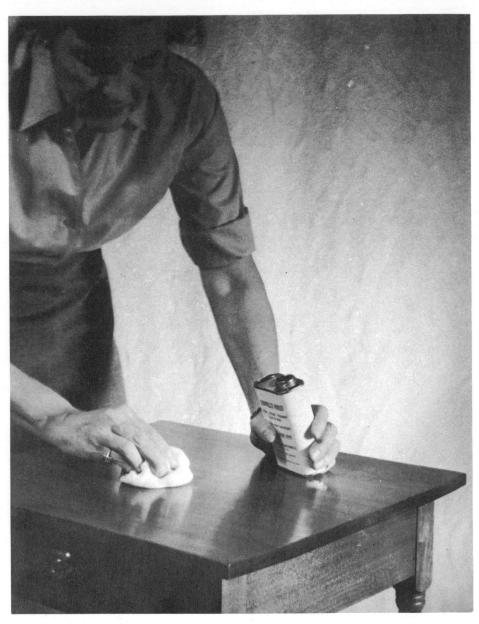

There Is No Greater Satisfaction Than Revealing the True
Beauty of Old Wood With An Appropriate Finish.

CARE OF FINISHED FURNITURE

There are any number of furniture polishes on the market. We believe the best polish and the least expensive can be made easily and quickly right at home. Simply use 75% lemon oil (real lemon oil, not so-called industrial finish) and 25% denatured alcohol. Shake well in the bottle and continue shaking to maintain an emulsion. Wipe surface with cheesecloth pad moistened with the polish. The alcohol removes dirt or film, the lemon oil polishes. Finish off by rubbing with a flannel type of cloth.

An over watered plant, the wet base of a cocktail glass, hot dishes, spilled perfume and toilet water results in milky white marks in the finish. These marks can be quickly removed with our product SANTASH. Stretch a close woven cloth, such as old sheeting, over the forefinger, moisten with SANTASH and rub the spot lightly. With reasonable care this will remove the spot but leave no dull mark in the finish.

Dark spots on finished furniture indicate, ordinarily, that heat or acid has gone through the finish and into the wood. In this case sanding, or even scraping, may be necessary (see Section IV, PREPARING THE SURFACE FOR FINISHING and Section VI, FINISHING WITH FARWELL'S FINEST).

Our personal preference is not for the use of wax. If used over our—or any finish—it has to be carefully removed if one wishes to add more finish or pad over a spot which has been repaired. If wax has been used and removal is necessary, we recommend carbon tetra chloride as much safer than the very combustible benzine.

Good furniture will stand a surprising amount of heat without being actually burned or charred. In cases where a fire is stopped before the flames reach the furniture, or when a heating plant back-fires, a black, thick and exceedingly sticky smoke film is deposited. From years of experience in appraisals of fire and smoke damage and supervision of restoration work we concocted a mixture which removes the smoke film but does not disturb the finish underneath. FARWELL'S SPECIAL CLEANER is rubbed over the surface with cheesecloth pads, once to remove the bulk of the film, a second time to remove all traces and leave a clean surface. Use plenty of pads, renewing them frequently, as they quickly become filled with the black, sticky covering.

"Before" and "After"—The Removal of the Dingy
Old Finish Now Reveals the Fine Inlay and
Grain of Old Cherry.

FRAMES

Restored chests of the light woods, such as pine, maple, and birch, often need a mirror to be hung over them. An attractive and appropriate frame can be made by picking up (at small cost, because they are quite common) an Empire ogee frame. These frames are mahogany veneer over pine. Remove the veneer, then finish (see Section VI, FINISHING) and you have an attractive, plain, honey-colored frame. The veneer is removed by first soaking off the outer layer of old finish with denatured alcohol. Then sink the frame in a bath tub of water as hot as it will run from the tap. Soaked over-night, the veneer can be started with an X-Acto knife blade and peeled off by hand. When dry, sand lightly before finishing.

With the tremendous interest in art, and with so many painting, there is need for a great number of frames. New frames are expensive. At sales, auctions, or in almost all attics, there are frames, well made but often horribly decorated, which can be picked up for a song. Many of these frames are made of gesso over wood, and fairly ornate. Missing or broken details can be filled in by making a clay impression of the same detail elsewhere on the frame. Do this with a lump of child's modeling clay. Sprinkle flour or face powder over the detail, press modeling clay carefully over the detail, and carefully work loose and remove. This impression is then filled with plaster of Paris mixed with water to a pouring consistency. When the mixture has dried hard, pull away the clay and you have the needed repair part. Fit this in and glue with cold plastic resin glue.

The ornate frames are made attractive and appropriate for the purpose intended by first painting them with flat white or ivory. When this is dry, brush on a glaze made of varnish and an oil color. Immediately wipe off with a cheesecloth pad, leaving more of the glaze in the deep parts and very little on the high parts.

31

Very attractive glazes can be made by the addition, from tubes of color, of burnt umber, cobalt or lighter blues, medium chrome green or Venetian red.

The high lights may be touched with pale gold bronzing powder or real gold leaf (see Section X, GILDING) if desired.

AN ATTRACTIVELY RESTORED GLAZE FINISHED FRAME
COMPLEMENTS THE WORK OF THE VERMONT ARTIST,
KATHERINE KING JOHNSON.

RESTORATION OF PIANO FINISHES WITH FARWELL'S FINEST

Older pianos were finely finished by craftsmen of great skill and devotion to the work. The result, after many coats of rubbing and finishing varnishes, was a final finish of real beauty and depth. This very depth, however, makes the finish more susceptible to checking and crazing, especially on the parts of the piano near a window and strong light. In this day and age, the cost of removing the entire finish and starting over is almost prohibitive.

We outline a method of restoring crazed finishes with our padding finish which can be done without moving the piano and by anyone who has an interest in the job and some patience. It is not difficult but it is time consuming. We urge that small areas be done at a time. With our method this can be done without showing "lap marks".

Move the piano a short way from the wall, protect the floor around and underneath with a tarpaulin, old quilt or newspapers.

First, clean the surface thoroughly to remove any traces of dirt or wax and furniture polish which may have been previously applied. Carbon tetra chloride is best, applied with a cheesecloth pad. Then slightly reduce the depth of the check marks by sanding, first with 2/o Open Kote sandpaper and then 220A soft back finishing paper. Then wipe the surface with a cheesecloth pad saturated with denatured alcohol. This removes all dust and slightly draws together the check marks.

Next, proceed to apply FARWELL'S FINEST as in finishing any piece of furniture (and just as directed on our label). Our finish gradually fills in the check marks. The finest results can be obtained by more than one rubbing with a light sanding in between with 220A soft back finishing paper. Since this can be done almost immediately after "rubbing up" a small area, the finish is a little soft and will quickly clog the paper. Have at hand a brass wire suede leather brush and keep the paper clear by brushing it. By doing this the paper will last a long time.

When the area is finished to your satisfaction let stand an hour and lightly go over it with a cheesecloth pad *very slightly* moistened with denatured alcohol. This will leave a very "high" finish (very shiny). If a slightly duller finish is desired, rub gently with 4/0 steel wool.

If, on edges or elsewhere, you go through the original finish and stain, obtain small amounts of Bismark Brown powder and Nigrosine black powder. In different proportions, these two aniline stains, when dissolved in alcohol, will give you any color from ebony to red mahogany or pale walnut or maple. The stain is applied with a small soft brush after the work of finishing is completed (the stain "takes into" our finish).

GILDING

This section is exclusively for those who like to fuss. Working with gold leaf requires a variety of materials and implements. It is necessary to have time and patience and, occasionally, to call down the wrath of the Lord upon a piece of gold leaf that flutters off in the wrong direction. But it is fascinating work. Gold is beautiful. The art of gold beating is the oldest profession (next to Mrs. Warren's!). Gold never tarnishes and no substitute has even been found to take its place.

Gold leaf is so thin that the slightest imperfection on the surface beneath it shows up. So preparing the surface to absolute smoothness is most important.

Over dry sanded wood, first put two or three coats of thin shellac to seal the wood properly. Do the same over repairs of wood or plaster of Paris (see Section VIII, FRAMES). Then build up a hard smooth surface by brushing on a mixture of gilder's whiting and glue size. Glue size is made by soaking two ounces of Rabbit Skin Glue flakes in a pint of water for one hour, then heating (but not boiling) it in a double boiler until the glue has completely dissolved. After each coat of the whiting and glue size mixture is brushed on and dried, sand smooth. At least three coats are necessary for a proper surface. The final coat should be sanded with a very fine grit sandpaper. Then brush on a coat of oil slow size. A fairly stiff brush should be used, taking care to cover every bit of the surface but leaving a thin even coat of sizing. Oil size usually comes in a yellow tone.

Gold leaf is so thin that the color of the undercoat affects the tone of the gilding. By adding cobalt blue from a tube of that color, one gets a green which gives an attractive, rather antique effect to the gold leaf. Oil size takes at least twenty four hours to reach the proper tackiness. This is called a "whistling tack". It may be tried out by applying a finger to the surface and withdrawing it quickly. This produces a sort of whistling snap if the tack is just right. The slow size holds its tack for hours, so the application of the gold leaf may be done unhurriedly. Most surfaces may be gilded with the so-called patent leaf. This is gold leaf mounted on paper. Appropriate sizes are cut with shears and applied by pressing on the paper side with the fingers. After some drying, the gold leaf may be further smoothed and burnished with a small ball of cotton batting. Carving and deep ornamentations have to be done by carefully placing a piece of gold leaf over a section to be gilded and gently pressing the gold leaf in with the hairs of a rabbit's foot. This gilding has to be done with the regular, unmounted leaf, not the patent leaf (see following paragraphs on handling gold leaf with a gilder's tip).

An interesting and attractive contrast, (on frames especially) is accomplished by burnishing (making very shiny) just the high spots of the ornamentation or the top of a raised panel. This is done by rubbing these spots with an agate burnisher. However, gold leaf will rub through when this is done unless there is an undercoat of burnishing clay. Burnishing clays come in yellow to give a lemon effect or in red and blue to give darker, richer tones to the gold. They are also used over larger surfaces covered with gilder's whiting and glue mixture when there is no intention of burnishing the whole surface with an agate.

The undercoating of burnishing clays is made by reducing them with water and mixing the reduced clay two parts to one part of Rabbit Skin Glue solution. This mixture is kept warm and brushed on with a fairly soft brush. As each coat drys it is fine sanded. The final coat is very fine sanded and then rubbed with a flannel type cloth. Use at least three coats. Then the final operation is to brush the surface with Rabbit Skin Glue solution, slightly let down with water.

To apply gold leaf (the unmounted) over burnishing clay, wet a small section with a mixture of 50% alcohol, 50% water, using a camel's hair brush. The alcohol works on the glue in the final coating and causes it to become tacky. The gold leaf is then carefully laid on with a gilder's tip and gently pressed down with a ball of cotton batting. After drying over night, such parts as may be desired can be burnished with an agate burnisher. (Patent gold leaf cannot be used successfully over burnishing clay.)

Handling regular gold leaf with a gilder's tip is tricky and sometimes exasperating. Pieces are cut off from the approximately 3″ x 3″ sheets by folding back the dividing piece of paper and then cutting the leaf to the size desired. A leaf cutting knife may be purchased but a very satisfactory home made tool is a hard wood knitting needle, the point of which has been slightly dulled with fine sandpaper.

Gilder's tips, as purchased, are wider than we like. We cut the cardboard mounting to shorter widths, binding the cut edges with masking tape. The hairs of the tip are run through one's own hair, then the tip is placed carefully on the gold leaf, carefully lifted and placed over the sized section. Capillary attraction draws the gold leaf from the tip to the piece you are gilding. It is then further fixed on by rabbit's foot or ball of cotton. During this process there should not be the slightest breath of air stirring, including your own breath. And woe be to the members of your household who, at this moment slam doors, stamp feet or inform you that you are wanted on the long distance telephone!

When it is all done and you, including your vocabulary of cuss words, are completely exhausted, there is real satisfaction. Someone says, "What a beautiful gilt frame!". You look up nonchalantly and reply, "Yes, it is rather attractive — 23 carat gold leaf, you know. Not much of a job when you are accustomed to doing it!"

VERMONT

There was a young man from Vermont
Who went to Boston, to visit his aunt.
Though she'd rave and she'd rant
He would call her "ant"
For an aunt is an "ant" (in Vermont)!

Of course all Vermont aunts are not "ants". We have many fine characters who have not gone forth "a kingly crown to gain" but whose talk is Back Bay Boston or the upper east side's Sutton Place. And we know those delightful folks who have come to ski, to hunt, to fish and finally decided that Vermont is a great place in which to live. Among them we hear traces of midwestern, Texas, tidewater Maryland, Philadelphia and even that most fascinating of all talk, the native language of some of our finest and most loyal college friends —pure Brooklynese.

Most of the fine antiques in Vermont have been brought here. John White made some fine step-down Windsors and the Baileys some graceful silver spoons. But, for the most part, when fine antiques were created Vermont was a wilderness. Many fine things were brought up here in ox-carts. In fact, we have been told of so many things coming by ox-cart we have wondered, if they all started at once, if there might have been need of ox traffic officers along the forest trails. But having arrived here, carried by our early Vermont families, or the good people who have arrived later, antiques are cherished and well cared for. And Vermonters are always glad to show them.

When we were very, very young, one of Vermont's great ladies sent us a picture of the Green Mountain Flyer coming up through Waterbury Notch under a full head of steam and white smoke billowing from her stack. With it was a poem predicting our adventures and our travels. It ends:

"And when at last you're back again
 Oh how your heart will thump
You'll doff your derby hat and bow
To dear old Camel's Hump".

We no longer possess a derby hat. But when we travel north and look across at her western slope, or when we drive to the top of Clay Hill in Montpelier and watch the sun set behind her, we do make our bow to Camel's Hump — and to Vermont!

WHERE TO PURCHASE

Item	*Stores*
Alcohol	Paint & Hardware
Agate Burnisher	Behlen*
Aniline stains	Behlen*
Brass suede leather brush	Chain
Burnishing clay	Behlen*
Colors in oil	Paint
Contact cement	Hardware
Child's modeling clay	Chain
Cold plastic resin glue	Hardware
Duritite	Hardware
Gold leaf	Artist supplies or Behlen*
Gilder's tip	Artist supplies or Behlen*
Half round file	Hardware
Plaster of Paris	Paint
Rabbit skin glue	Behlen*
Sandpaper	Hardware
Steelwool	Hardware
Woods (exotic and veneers)	Constantine**
X-Acto knives	Hardware

*H. Behlen & Bro., Inc., 10 Christopher St., New York City

**Albert Constantine & Son, Inc., 2050 Eastchester Road, New York City (61)

SPECIAL: Rabbit's Foot (for gilding). First catch your rabbit. If you can't, write us and we will get you one (a foot, we mean, not a whole rabbit).

NOTES

NOTES

NOTES

NOTES